Got It!

A Game for
Building Vocabulary
and Conversation

Phyllis Gardner

PRO LINGUA ⬤ ASSOCIATES

Pro Lingua Associates
PO Box 1348
Brattleboro, Vermont 05302 USA
Office 802-257-7779
Orders: 800-366-4775
Email: info@ProLinguaAssociates.com
WebStore www.ProLinguaAssociates.com
SAN: 216-0579

At **Pro Lingua**
our objective is to foster an approach
to learning and teaching that we call
interplay, the **inter**action of language
learners and teachers with their materials,
with the language and culture,
and with each other in active, creative,
and productive **play.**

This book was designed and set by Arthur A. Burrows using the sans-serif typeface Candara, developed in 2005 for Microsoft by Gary Munch and published by Ascender. Sans-serif faces often appear to be stiff and mechanical, and though easy to read in short texts, they lack grace. This face, designed for digital reading, is said to be friendly, playful, and humanist. The letter shapes are open; the lines subtly flared. It is elegant when used for display or in small phrases, but comfortable to read in extended text. The photographs are from Dreamstime.com Agency: front cover image © Bymandesigns, title page © Madrabothair, page viii © Diego Vito Cervo, page 87 left © Darrinhenry, right © Monkey Business Images, and back cover © Photographerlondon.

The book was printed and bound by Royal Palm Press in Punto Gorda, Florida.

Printed in the United States of America
First edition, second printing 2016

Contents

Contents

✺ Introduction ✺

Got It! is a fun and creative game suitable for ESOL students at any level (elementary to adult) and of any degree of proficiency. It can be played as a filler in those spare minutes at class end, or more comprehensively as an entire lesson. There is no prep for the teacher and answers are provided. The game is played consistently the same way, so once you've 'got it' (and it's easy), you can just whip out the cards.

Got It! is primarily intended as a vocabulary builder, and uses as its base standard vocabulary as well as questions inspiring more creative and thoughtful answers. Words and ideas are brainstormed in groups in a game setting, and because the students themselves are generating ideas, and communicating, the potential for vocabulary acqustion is high. This can be capitalized on by supplementing the game with activities that provide for expanded vocabulary and writing practice.

Though the game generates thought and excitement, the noise factor is low as students are reminded to keep their voices down lest another group steal their ideas. Time permitting, play just one subtopic or the entire page.

The Layout

The first section of the book consists of 40 pages, each with a topic and four subtopics, two Easy and two Hard. If you browse through the topics and answers, you will note that some topics are more standard and others more creative. Here's an example of a page:

Each of the subtopics is called a "card." The second half of the book contains an Answer Key for each of the subtopic cards. The key is not intended to give THE answers for each subtopic; it is simply a collection of prossible answers that can be used in a variety of ways to follow up on the game. Of course, students often supply answers that are original and "out of the box."

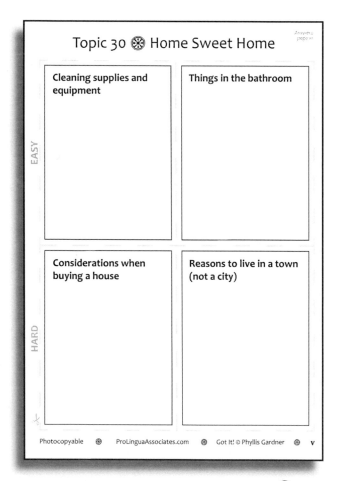

Topic 30 ✺ Home Sweet Home

EASY

Cleaning supplies and equipment

Things in the bathroom

HARD

Considerations when buying a house

Reasons to live in a town (not a city)

Photocopyable ✺ ProLinguaAssociates.com ✺ Got It! © Phyllis Gardner ✺ v

How It's Played

After choosing a topic, write the topic on the board or make photocopies of the page – one copy for each group. At this point you can use the page in two ways. You can give the group the whole page and tell them which subtopic card they will do. Alternatively, cut out one of the subtopics and give it to each group.

Place the students in groups of four (more or less). The groups can be of the same ability or mixed ability. Then tell them:

❀ "We will do subtopic card *Tools*. All of you will have the same card. In your group you will help each other to come up with words and phrases (hammer, saw) that are relevant to the subtopic on your card.

❀ Write as many as you can in the time given. One person will be the Writer and write your answers on the card (or a separate piece of paper). Don't worry about spelling.

❀ Don't talk too loudly or the other groups will hear your answers!" (Hand out cards.) "Ready? Go!"

❀ "Bzzz – time's up!" (The length of time allotted to generate answers will vary depending on the complexity and number of possible answers.)

❀ "Okay, Group One, Mariana, please be the Reader. Read your answers, and all the other groups look at your list to see if you've got the same answer."

❀ Mariana reads "screwdriver" and Group Two and Group Four have it, too. They say, "Got It!" and all groups who have it, including Mariana's, cross it off their lists.

❀ When Group One is done reading their list, their score will reflect how many items they had that no other group had.

❀ Keep track of scores on the board. Do the same procedure for each of the remaining groups, asking, "What words did you have that they didn't?"

❀ The group with the most points wins, candy for them. You can then supplement their answers with the suggested ones found in the Answer Section.
NOTE: As the referee, you may have to disqualify answers that are irrelevant to the subtopic.

On Multi-level Groups

While multi-level classes present challenges, *Got It!*, like any team-based exercise, facilitates the process of language learning. A higher-level student has the role of Writer, an intermediate is Reader, and a beginner scans the list. When students hear a word, they cross it out and call, "Got it!" Because there are both Easy and Hard topics, you can use cards appropriate to your students' proficiency. The use of a picture dictionary facilitates comprehension for all and helps to equalize the playing field. See page 83 for suggestions for doing so.

Expanding Your Topics Collection

After using this Got It! activity for many years, I have a large collection of topics. On page 41, I have added a list of 24 extra topics that I know work well. However, I encourage you to choose your own; you know your students, and the best topics are those that reflect their interests and needs. On page 82 there is a blank topic sheet (Topic 0). Copy it, create your own topic and subtopics, and you've really got it!

Expanding the Game to Other Activities

In the back of the book, beginning on page 83, are suggestions for alternative and additional activities that will maximize the use of the games.

A Parting Word or Two

Language learning is enhanced when infused with a bit of fun. I've played **Got It!** with ESOL students for years with continued success; they 'get into' it, have fun with it, communicate, and develop a curiosity about the meanings of words. Have fun! – *PG*

To Betsy Mathias for "all you do" for RARE
– you are the heart of us.
And to our hardworking teachers who care.

Topic 1 ✳ Keeping Up Appearances

Answers
page 42

What women can do with their hair

Things in the toiletries aisle

EASY

How you know you are reaching middle age

Bad habits

HARD

Topic 2 ✸ Social Butterfly

EASY

Comings and goings (greetings)	Places and ways to socialize

HARD

Occasions for sending someone a greeting card	Things associated with a wedding

Answers
page 44

EASY

People in uniform

People who work at night

HARD

Jobs for teenagers

Occupations A-F

Answers
page 45

Tools	Jobs men typically do

EASY

What you should and shouldn't do on a job interview	Reasons for quitting your job

HARD

American breakfast foods

Fruit

EASY

Popular sandwiches

Kinds of bread

HARD

Answers
page 47

EASY

Spices and herbs

**Appliances and things in the kitchen
(not inside drawers or cabinets)**

HARD

Cooking terms and processes

What you can do to/with an egg

Topic 7 ✺ Yum!

EASY

Desserts	Standard ice cream flavors

HARD

Things associated with a restaurant (what you do and eat)	Fast food "restaurants"

EASY

Beverages

Foods that begin with "P"

HARD

Crunchy food

Fruits with peels/rinds you don't eat

Answers
page 50

EASY

Places with long or slow lines	**Things you want to arrive on time for**
Countries that start with "S"	**Things at the playground or park**

HARD

Answers
page 51

EASY

Things associated with summer

Bad-weather clothing

HARD

Weather terms

Natural disasters

EASY

Things in a medicine cabinet

What doctors tell patients not to do

HARD

Kinds of doctors/specialists

At the dentist's

Answers
page 53

EASY

Cold/flu symptoms

Medical reasons to stay home from work or school

HARD

Itchy things

Things people are afraid of

Answers
page 54

EASY

Parts of the body - the head

Body movements

HARD

Inside the body

What you need both hands for

Answers
page 55

EASY

Things that give light	Things that you use water for

HARD

Things with holes	Things that are round or circular

Answers
page 56

EASY

Things that melt or dissolve

Things that come in pairs

HARD

**Things that go together,
like "salt & pepper"**

Things that go up and down

Topic 16 ✳ Keeping Busy

Answers
page 57

EASY

Household chores	Weekend activites

HARD

Places to go for entertainment and relaxation	Hobbies and crafts

Answers
page 58

EASY

American holidays	Things associated with Thanksgiving

HARD

Things associated with Washington, D.C.	Things associated with Alaska

Answers
page 59

EASY

Tourist attractions in the U.S.

Large U.S. corporations

HARD

States with 9 or more letters

Things associated with cowboys

EASY

| U.S. States | U.S. cities (best known) |

HARD

| Mountains, rivers, deserts, and lakes | States along the coasts |

Topic 20 ✳ Can You Turn It Down? (Music and the Media)

EASY

Kinds/genres of music	Famous American popular singers (living)

HARD

Musical instruments	Kinds of TV shows or movies (some may apply to both)

Answers page 62

EASY

Animal sounds

Animals at the zoo

HARD

Animals you avoid

Animal parts that people don't have

Answers page 63

EASY

| Pets | What dogs hate and what they love |

HARD

| Reasons to put a dog in obedience school | How people treat dogs like humans |

EASY

Sports played with a ball

Sports played without a ball

HARD

Olympic sports

Water and snow sports

Topic 24 ✳ What Smells Funny? (The Senses)

EASY

The colors you see	What you smell, nice or not

HARD

Things that feel soft	Textures

Things you see that are red

Things that are hot

EASY

Things that feel sticky

Places and things that are noisy

HARD

Answers
page 67

EASY

Words associated with a classroom	School subjects

HARD

Kinds of schools	Rooms and places at school

*Answers
page 68*

EASY

Words that end in -TION

Words that rhyme with "FIGHT"

HARD

**Other words for "GREAT,"
as in "That was a great movie."**

Words that rhyme with "YOU"

Answers
page 69

EASY

Words that begin with BR-

Opposites (big/little)

HARD

Verbs with "UP"

Punctuation marks

EASY

Abbreviations

Regular past tense -ed   sounds of t/d/id

HARD

Irregular past participles with "have/has" such as "have gone" (different from past tense)

Adjectives that end with -LESS

Answers
page 71

EASY

| **Cleaning supplies and equipment** | **Things in the bathroom** |

HARD

| **Considerations when buying a house** | **Reasons to live in a town (not a city)** |

Answers
page 72

EASY

What families save money for	Family members

HARD

The most important things to look for in a marriage/relationship	What couples argue about

Answers
page 73

EASY

Toys

What you do with a baby

HARD

What a child wants before bed
Why they wake their parents

What kids don't like or are scared of

Answers
page 74

EASY

Stores	Things at a mall that are not stores

HARD

Places that offer services	What comes in a box, a jar, or a can

Answers
page 75

EASY

Terms for giving directions

Types of vehicles with wheels

HARD

Kinds of transportation without wheels

What people don't like about flying

Topic 35 ✲ The Well-Dressed Man

Answers page 76

What you wear or take to the beach

Bad-weather wear

Kinds of shoes

Fabrics and materials

EASY

Adjectives that describe people physically

Adjectives that describe food

HARD

Positive and negative adjectives that describe people's personalities

Positive and negative adjectives that describe emotions – How do you feel?

EASY

What you can get a traffic ticket for	Important documents and cards

HARD

Crimes	Phrases and words associated with a courtroom

Topic 38 ✸ The Great Outdoors

EASY

What you see when you look up

What people do in their backyards

HARD

Flowers and trees

Things outside a house and in the yard

Topic 39 ✺ Around the World

Answers
page 80

Languages

European countries

International capital cities

Countries ending with -LAND

EASY

HARD

Answers
page 81

EASY

What parents remind or encourage their children to do

Things made of plastic

HARD

Things that have changed since Grandma's time

Objects and events that bring good and bad luck

✳ Extra Topics ✳

Easy	▦	Things made of metal
Easy	▦	Places that deliver things
Easy	▦	Things you change
Easy	▦	Things that are fake
Easy	▦	Things you eat with a spoon
Easy	▦	Things in a parade
Easy	▦	What little kids are told not to play with
Easy	▦	Baseball and football teams
Easy	▦	Furniture
Easy	▦	Road/traffic Signs
Easy	▦	Car manufacturers
Hard	▦	Jobs where you can get wet
Hard	▦	Something a millionaire would own or have
Hard	▦	Jobs where you need your head covered
Hard	▦	Things you use your index finger/thumb for
Hard	▦	Things you spray out of a can
Hard	▦	Things women spend more time doing than men
Hard	▦	National parks
Hard	▦	Insects
Hard	▦	What baby animals are called
Hard	▦	People you call to fix things and beautify your house
Hard	▦	Vehicles where you sit in back
Hard	▦	Halloween costumes
Hard	▦	Birthstones

Topic 1 ✳ Keeping Up Appearances
Possible Answers

What women can do with their hair

get haircut, shampoo, condition, blow dry, comb, brush, dye, highlight, cut, style, layer, shape, curl/perm, straighten, make bangs, make ponytail, braid, put it up

Things in the toiletries aisle

blush, body lotion, bubble bath, comb, cotton balls/swab, deodorant, ear drops, eye drops, eye wash, face cleanser, floss, hair brush, hair dye, moisturizer, mouthwash, nail clippers, nail file, nail polish/remover, razor/blade, shampoo, shaving cream, soap, sunblock, tissues, toothbrush, tweezers

How you know you are reaching middle age

wrinkles, balding/thinning hair, weight gain, sagging/flabby body, gray/white/silver hair, dye your hair, become forgetful, joints ache/stiff, become less active/tired/fatigued, need reading glasses, hot flashes

Bad habits

nail biting, being late, spitting, cursing/swearing, cracking knuckles, littering, picking one's nose, skipping breakfast, snacking, overeating, eating too fast, chewing with mouth open, smoking, not washing hands after bathroom, exaggerating, stealing, watching too much TV, texting constantly, being messy, being a slob

EASY

HARD

Topic 2 ✳ Social Butterfly
Possible Answers

EASY

Comings and goings (greetings)

Comings: shake hands, hug, kiss, pat on back

Formal: hello, how are you (doing), how do you do, nice to see/meet you, how's the family, what have you been up to, good morning/afternoon/evening

Informal: hi, how ya doin', how's it going, what's happening, what's up, yo, howdy, hey, hiya

Goings:
Formal: take care, it was nice/great seeing/talking to you, good night, be well, goodbye, give my best (regards) to…

Informal: bye, bye bye, see ya, take it easy, see you later (alligator), hasta la vista, night, g'night

Places and ways to socialize

Places: club, coffee shop, neighbor's house, backyard fence, the gym, church/temple/mosque, bar, disco, dance, college dorm, a dog park, a retreat

Ways: have a party, play party games, volunteer, take a class, play a sport, use Facebook and other social media

HARD

Occasions for sending someone a greeting card

birthday, anniversary, Valentine's Day, graduation/commencement, Christmas/Chanukah/Kwanzaa, condolences/sympathy, wedding/marriage, thank you, sweet 16, bar mitzvah, congratulations, thinking of you, National Adoption Day

Things associated with a wedding

bride, groom, bridesmaids, best man, ring bearer, flower girl, church/chapel/synagogue/temple/mosque, service/ceremony, rings, vows, kiss, priest/minister/rabbi/justice of the peace, elopement, Las Vegas, gown, veil, invitations, flowers, reception, dancing, food, wedding cake, toast, bouquet, flowers, music/band/organist, limo, honeymoon, gifts, newlyweds, husband and wife

EASY

People in uniform

astronaut, bus driver, ship's captain, cheerleader, doctor, nurse, doorman, military personnel (soldier, sailor), firefighter, police officer, judge, park ranger, parochial school student, airline personnel, pilot, referee, umpire, postal/mail carrier/clerk, sports team player, waiter/waitress/server

People who work at night

ambulance driver, baker, casino worker, janitor/custodian, musician, nurse, pilot, convenience store worker, doctor, prostitute/hooker, theater people, doorman, taxi driver, EMT (emergency medical technician), factory worker, firefighter, police officer, prison guard

HARD

Reasons for quitting your job

bad boss, low salary, no benefits, no promotion, don't like job, poor schedule (not enough/too many hours), don't get along with coworkers, too far away, too much traffic, moved away, got a better job, decided to go back to school, got pregnant, sexual harassment, illness, disability, retirement, personal issues, won lottery

Occupations A-F

accountant, actor/actress, administrative assistant, appliance repair person, architect, artist, auto mechanic, babysitter, baker, barber, beautician, bus driver, business man/woman, butcher, carpenter, cashier, chef, chiropractor, cleaning woman, construction worker, computer technician, customer service rep, custodian, day care worker, delivery person, dentist, dental hygienist, detective, doctor, editor, electrician, engineer, factory worker, farmer, firefighter, fisherman, florist, foreman

Possible Answers

Tools

ax, chisel, clamp, drill, hammer, square, staple gun, tape measure, plane, pliers, sander, saw, screwdriver, vise, wire cutters, wrench

---

Jobs men typically do

astronaut, auto mechanic, carpenter, chef, coal miner, construction worker, electrician, farmer, father, fireman, demolition worker, drill sergeant, lumberjack, race car driver, roofing, fisherman, football player, janitor/custodian, lawn mover/landscaper, sanitation worker (trash), truck driver

---

EASY

HARD

What you should and shouldn't do at a job interview

Should: dress neatly and appropriately, be on time/punctual, prepare for the interview, be familiar with the company, greet the interviewer, shake hands, make eye contact, listen carefully, ask questions, talk about your skills, qualifications, and experience, thank the interviewer, write a thank-you note.

Shouldn't: be late, have cell phone on, chew gum, call interviewer by first name (unless requested), interrupt, badmouth last boss

---

Jobs for teenagers

restaurant worker (busboy, dishwasher), do yard work, mow lawn, shovel snow, babysitter, lifeguard, supermarket – bagger/cashier/gather shopping carts, fast-food restaurant worker, newspaper route, delivery boy (pizza, Chinese food), camp counselor, pet sitting, dog walking, wash cars, golf caddy

---

EASY

American breakfast foods

bacon, bagel, cereal, danish, eggs, French toast, granola, ham, home fries, muffins, oatmeal, pancakes, sausage, toast, waffles

Fruit

apple, peach, pear, apricot, plum, prune, avocado, banana, berries (blackberry, blueberry, raspberry, strawberry), grapefruit, kiwi, lemon, lime, mango, melon (cantaloupe, honeydew, watermelon), nectarine, cherry, coconut, date, fig, grape, orange (tangerine, clementine), pineapple

HARD

Popular sandwiches

cheese/bacon/ham, egg salad, grilled cheese, ham and cheese, roast beef, tuna, BLT (bacon, lettuce, & tomato), Philadelphia cheese steak, hero/hoagie/ grinder/poorboy/sub (submarine), peanut butter and jelly, turkey

Kinds of bread

white, wheat, whole grain, rye, pumpernickel, sourdough, gluten free, cinnamon raisin, corn bread, muffin, tortilla, pita, bagel, baguette, biscuit, bun, roll, croissant, naan, sweet roll

Topic 6 ✸ Can You Cook?
Possible Answers

EASY

Spices and herbs

basil, bay leaf, cilantro, cinnamon, cloves, coriander, curry, dill, garlic powder, ginger, mint, mustard, nutmeg, onion, oregano, paprika, parsley, sage, tarragon, thyme, turmeric

Appliances and things in the kitchen (not inside drawers or cabinets)

cabinets, coffee maker, cookbooks, counter, dish towel, dishwasher, electric can opener, garbage disposal, garbage pail, microwave, paper towel holder, refrigerator/freezer, sink, stove/oven, spice rack, tea kettle, toaster oven, trash compactor

HARD

Cooking terms and processes

cut, chop, slice, grate, peel, break, beat, stir, pour, add, combine, mix, cook, bake, boil, broil, steam, fry, sauté, simmer, roast, barbecue/grill, stir fry, microwave (nuke)

What you can do to/with an egg

break/crack, peel it, scramble it, separate yolks from white, beat, make meringue from whites, color/ decorate/hide/ hunt/roll Easter eggs, make egg salad, drink raw in energy drink, make a cake, make pancakes, french toast, have an egg fight, race with egg on spoon, raise chickens

How to prepare it:
hard/soft boiled, fried (over easy, sunny side up), deviled, poached, omelet, scrambled, eggs Benedict

EASY

Desserts

baklava, biscotti, brownies, cake,
cannoli, cobbler, cookies, cupcakes,
doughnuts, éclair, fruit, fudge,
ice cream, pie, mousse, pudding

Standard ice cream flavors

butter pecan, cherry vanilla, chocolate,
chocolate chip, coffee, cookie dough,
cookies & cream, maple walnut,
mint chip, peach, pistachio,
rum raisin, strawberry, vanilla

HARD

**Things associated with a restaurant
(what you do and eat)**

Do: make a reservation/book a table,
look at menu, order, beckon waiter,
eat, ask for the check, pay, leave a tip,
have a drink, relax, converse, dine

Eat: appetizer, entree/main course,
salad, sides, drinks/beverages, dessert

Fast-food "restaurants"

Arby's, Burger King, Chipotle,
Dairy Queen, Domino's Pizza,
Dunkin Donuts, El Pollo Loco, Five Guys,
Jamba Juice, KFC, Long John Silver,
McDonalds, Panda Express, Panera,
Pizza Hut, Popeyes, Quiznos,
Roy Rogers, Smoothie King, Subway,
Taco Bell, Wendy's

Possible Answers

EASY

Beverages

beer, ale, cider, tea, coffee, chai, water, cocoa/hot chocolate, soda, wine, juice (apple, grape, grapefruit, orange, tomato), lemonade, milk

Foods that begin with "P"

pancakes, panini, papaya, pasta, peanuts, peanut butter, peas, pesto, pickles, pie, pineapple, pistachios, pizza, plum, popcorn, potatoes, potato chips, prunes, pudding, pumpkin

HARD

Crunchy food

apple, biscotti, carrots, celery, cereal, chips, crackers, granola bars, pickles, popcorn, pretzels, toast, fried chicken

Fruits with peels/rinds you don't eat

avocado, banana, coconut, grapefruit, lemon, lime, lychee, melon (cantaloupe, honeydew, watermelon), orange, papaya, pineapple, pomegranate

EASY

Places with long or slow lines

check out at supermarket, the post office, DMV (Dept. of Motor Vehicles), ladies' room, rush hour traffic, Disneyland, polling (voting) booth, airport security line, the bank, Black Friday sales, passport bureau, toll booths, getting into a club, wait list at restaurants on weekends

Things you want to arrive on time for

funeral, (your own) wedding, job interview, your first day at work, dinner invitation, movie, the theater, court, church, class, test, surprise party, airplane flight, doctor's appointment, cruise, restaurant reservations, surgery

HARD

Countries that start with "S"

Samoa, Saudi Arabia, Senegal, Serbia, Seychelles, Sierra Leone, Singapore, Slovakia, Slovenia, Somalia, South Africa, South Korea, South Sudan, Spain, Sri Lanka, Sweden, Switzerland, Sudan, Suriname, Syria

Things at the playground or park

duck pond, picnic area, picnic table, grill, water fountain, fountain, bench, playground equipment - swing set, slide, seesaw, monkey bars, jungle gym, climbing equipment, sandbox, bike path, jogging path, track, trash can, tennis court, ball field, skateboard, roller/ice/inline skates

Possible Answers

Things associated with summer

heat/humidity/sun, beach, swimming, suntan/sunburn/sunscreen, pool, flip flops/sandals, bathing suit, shorts, tank tops, no school, ice cream, camping, watermelon, bees/wasps/yellow jackets/mosquitoes/fireflies, fishing, boating, July 4, AC/air conditioning/fans, lawn mowing, drive-in movies, vacation

Bad-weather clothing

coat, (down) (ski) jacket, windbreaker, raincoat, trench coat, poncho, vest, ski hat, rain hat, scarf, umbrella, boots, gloves, mittens, ear muffs, leggings, sweat pants/shirt, hood

Weather terms

sunny, warm, hot, heat, humid, muggy, clear, mild, cloudy, hazy, foggy, rainy, drizzle, shower, pouring, cool, cold, freezing, snow, hail, sleet, ice, windy, breezy, thunderstorm, lightning, thunder

Natural disasters

drought, famine, blizzard, hurricane/cyclone, tornado, earthquake, avalanche, tsunami/tidal wave, flood, wildfire, epidemic, heat wave, lightning strike, landslide/mudslide

EASY

HARD

EASY

Things in a medicine cabinet

antacid, aspirin, bandaids, bandage, cold tablets, cough drops/syrup, throat lozenges, decongestant/nasal spray, tooth paste, eye drops, gauze, ointment, vitamins, prescription medicine, sunscreen

What doctors tell patients not to do

smoke, eat fatty food/too much salt/ sweets/junk food, get stressed, not exercise, drink to excess, be overweight/obese

HARD

Kinds of doctors/specialists

acupuncturist, allergist, anesthesiologist, cardiologist, chiropractor, ENT (ear, nose and throat), gynecologist/obstetrician, internist, ophthalmologist, orthodontist, orthopedist, pediatrician, podiatrist, psychiatrist, surgeon

Things associated with going to the dentist

the dentist, dental assistant, hygienist, oral surgeon, orthodontist, braces, toothache, cap, crown, bridge, exam, cleaning, cavity, decay, abscess, filling, drill, shot, novocaine, gas, checkup, extract/pull, root canal, wisdom tooth, x-ray

Possible Answers

Cold/flu symptoms

runny nose, sneezing, congestion/stuffy nose, cough, sore throat, headache, fever, achy, chills, fatigue, nausea, vomiting, diarrhea

Medical reasons to stay home from work or school

headache, earache, toothache, stomachache, backache, sore throat, cough, chills, cramps, diarrhea, fever, laryngitis, infection, dizzy, nauseous/vomiting, wheezing/asthma, sprain, broken bone, strep throat, measles, mumps, chicken pox, mono, pneumonia

Itchy things

chicken pox, poison ivy/oak, dry skin, rash, wool sweater, bed bugs, mosquito/spider/flea bites, lice, eczema, psoriasis, peeling sunburn, hives, allergies/allergic reaction, cut grass, athlete's foot

Things people are afraid of

heights, small spaces (claustrophobia), crowds, flying, public speaking, spiders, snakes, dying, the dentist, being alone, falling, germs, commitment, rejection, failure, being abandoned

Children - monsters, boogey man, the dark, thunder, dogs, getting a shot (injection)

EASY

HARD

Topic 13 ✻ Your Body
Possible Answers

Parts of the body - the head

hair, forehead, eyebrow, eyelash, eyelid, eye, pupil, eyeball, temple, ear, earlobe, cheek, nose, nostril, mouth, lips, tongue, teeth, jaw, chin, face

Body movements

bend, bite, blink, chew, crawl, flex, hop, jump, nod, open/close (mouth), raise/lower, roll, run, sit, shrug, skip, smile, grin, frown, spin, squat, stand, twist, walk, wiggle, yawn

Inside the body

arteries, bladder, bones, brain, gallbladder, heart, intestines, kidney, liver, lungs, muscles, pancreas, pelvis, rib cage, skull, spine, stomach, throat

What you need both hands for

clap, applaud, diaper/bathe baby, tie shoes, get dressed, put on a belt, type fast, shovel snow, give a back rub/ massage, wash the dog, juggle, make pottery, play pattycake, fold laundry, climb a tree, knit, make a knot, wash the dishes

EASY

Things that give light

light bulb, lamp, flashlight, torch, lit candle, the sun, the moon, firefly, car headlight, street light, lightning, lit fireplace, refrigerator light, nightlight, Christmas light, fireworks

Things you use water for

drinking, bathing, showering, watering plants/lawn, gardening, brushing teeth, cooking spaghetti, putting in fish tank, flushing the toilet, making baby formula, washing hands, filling a pool, baptizing an infant, running the dishwasher, filling a washing machine, swimming, boating, a fountain

HARD

Things with holes

rings, beads, donuts, lifesavers, Cheerios, fruit loops, bagels, Swiss cheese, onion rings, bundt cake, penne, ziti, Spaghetti-o's, macaroni, canned pineapple, pitted olives, colander, pool table, sponge, honeycomb, straw, golf course, lace

Things that are round or circular

Round: ball, marble, balloon, globe, planet, orange, grape, blueberry

Circular: coin, bowl rim, pot lid, ring, clock, wheel, tire, frisbee, hula hoop, plate, CD, DVD, button, zero, bagel, donut, pizza pie, oreo cookie

EASY

Things that melt or dissolve

chocolate, lozenges in your mouth, sugar in water or heat, salt, food dye in water, chocolate syrup in milk, instant coffee, ice, butter, ice cream, sorbet, sherbet, frozen yogurt, plastic in heat, snow, CD in a hot car, wax candle, snowman, the witch in *The Wizard of Oz*

Things that come in pairs

shoes, socks, gloves, mittens, earrings, dice, crutches, contact lenses, skis, windshield wipers, headlights, cufflinks, chopsticks, twins, hands, eyes, ears, arms, legs, feet, lovebirds, wings, animals on Noah's Ark, handcuffs

HARD

Things that go together, like "salt & pepper"

pie & ice cream, suit & tie, chips & dip, Adam & Eve, spaghetti & meatballs, steak/meat & potatoes, ham & cheese, red beans & rice, knife, fork, & spoon, red, white, & blue, milk & cookies, bread & butter, bacon & eggs, mac & cheese, cereal & milk, shoes & socks, peaches & cream, rum & coke, washer & dryer, cheese & crackers, day & night, love & marriage, horse & carriage, cream & sugar

Things that go up and down

garage door, window, jack in thebox, elevator, escalator, temperature, seesaw, airplane, bouncing ball, volleyball, tennis ball, football, basketball, moods, rollercoaster, ferris wheel, piston, jackhammer, pogo stick, yo-yo, shades, the stock market, the economy, polls, tapping finger, person on trampoline, water cycle, nodding head

EASY

Household chores

do the laundry, change the sheets, make the bed, do/wash the dishes, straighten up, pick up, put away, organize, dust, polish/wax the furniture, sweep, vacuum, mop, take out the garbage, clean the bathroom, run the dishwasher

Weekend activites

watch TV, listen to the radio, read a book, listen to music, go to a concert, movie, or play, play a game, play cards, play/watch a sport, exercise, garden, use the computer, write a letter, relax, sleep late, visit, bathe, go to church, temple, mosque, talk on the phone, do errands, catch up on housework, eat out

HARD

Places to go for entertainment and relaxation

amusement park, carnival, circus, concert hall, dinner theater, disco, magic show, movies, pool hall, nightclub, theater, arcade, museum, art gallery, craft fair, yard sale, flea market, park, beach, mountains, aquarium, planetarium, zoo, bowling alley, opera, ballet, sporting event/stadium, horse race, car race, casino

Hobbies and crafts

collecting stamps/dolls/butterflies/coins/rocks/antiques

aquarium, gardening, painting, model (airplane) building, pottery, woodworking, bird watching, scrapbook, photography, astronomy, kite flying, sewing, needlepoint, knitting, crochet

EASY

American holidays

New Year's Day, Martin Luther King, Jr. Day, Presidents Day, Valentine's Day, Easter, Earth Day, Mother's Day, Memorial Day, Father's Day, Independence Day/July 4th, Labor Day, Columbus Day, Halloween, Veterans Day, Election Day, Thanksgiving, Christmas

Things associated with Thanksgiving

turkey, ham, stuffing, sweet potatoes/ yams, mashed potatoes, cranberry sauce, pumpkin pie, overeating, family, Macy's parade, football games, travel

HARD

Things associated with Washington, D.C.

White House, Washington Monument, Lincoln Monument, War Memorials – Vietnam/ Korean/ World War II, the Capitol, the Mall, Smithsonian museums, tourists, the Pentagon, politicians – President/senators/ congressmen

Things associated with Alaska

largest state, Arctic, huge, wilderness, Sarah Palin, wildlife – wolves/moose/ polar bears/grizzly bears/ salmon/ whales, 6 months darkness, Denali Park, dogsled, huskies, Eskimos, igloo, Inuit, Anchorage, Fairbanks, oil/gas/fishing industries, purchased from Russia (for two cents an acre), Gold Rush

Topic 18 ✹ Only in America

Possible Answers

EASY

Tourist attractions in the U.S.

Disneyland/World, Niagara Falls, Manhattan, Statue of Liberty, Empire State Building, Times Square, Broadway, Hollywood, White House, Las Vegas, San Francisco, Golden Gate Bridge, Grand Canyon, Yellowstone, other national parks

Large U.S. corporations

Walmart, Exxon, Mobil, Chevron, Phillips 66, Berkshire Hathaway, Apple, General Motors, General Electric, Valero Energy, Ford, Texaco, Amoco, Shell, IBM, Boeing, Dow Chemical, Xerox, Kraft, Google, Amazon

HARD

States with 9 or more letters

California, Connecticut, Louisiana, Massachusetts, Minnesota, Mississippi, New Hampshire, New Jersey, New Mexico, North/South Carolina, North/South Dakota, Pennsylvania, Rhode Island, Tennessee, Washington, West Virginia

Things associated with cowboys

American Indians, John Wayne, horses, spurs, chaps, the Wild West, 10-gallon hat, cowboy shirt, jeans, cowboy boots, rodeo, bull roping, lariat, cattle, guns, shootout, saloon, ranches, sleeping outdoors, campfires

Topic 19 ✻ Who's Good at U.S. Geography?
Possible Answers

EASY

U.S. States

Alabama, Alaska, Arizona, Arkansas, California, Colorado, Connecticut, Delaware, Florida, Georgia, Hawaii, Idaho, Illinois, Indiana, Iowa, Kansas, Kentucky, Louisiana, Maine, Maryland, Massachusetts, Michigan, Minnesota, Mississippi, Missouri, Montana, Nebraska, Nevada, New Hampshire, New Jersey, New Mexico, New York, North Carolina, North Dakota, Ohio, Oklahoma, Oregon, Pennsylvania, Rhode Island, South Carolina, South Dakota, Tennessee, Texas, Utah, Vermont, Virginia, Washington, West Virginia, Wisconsin, Wyoming

U.S. cities (best known)

NYC, NY; Los Angeles/San Francisco/ San Diego/San Jose, CA; Chicago, IL; Houston/Dallas, TX; Detroit, MI; Phoenix, AZ; Baltimore, MD; Columbus/Cleveland, OH; Memphis, TN; Washington, D.C.; Boston, MA; Seattle, WA; Denver, CO; Atlanta, GA; Minneapolis, MN; Honolulu, HI; Philadelphia, PA; Miami, FL; New Orleans, LA

HARD

Mountains, Rivers, Deserts and Lakes

Mountains: Adirondacks, Rocky Mts., Appalachians, Sierra Nevadas, Rainier, Mount Saint Helens, Cascades

Deserts: Death Valley, Mojave, Sonoran

Rivers: Rio Grande, Mississippi, Missouri, Delaware, Connecticut, Columbia, Colorado, Hudson, Snake

Lakes: Great Lakes (Ontario, Erie, Huron, Michigan, Superior), Great Salt Lake

States along the coast

East coast: Maine, New Hampshire, Massachusetts, Rhode Island, Connecticut, New York, New Jersey, Delaware, Maryland, Virginia, North Carolina, South Carolina, Georgia, Florida

West coast: California, Oregon, Washington

Gulf coast: Florida, Alabama, Mississippi, Louisiana, Texas

EASY

Kinds/genres of music

bluegrass, classical, reggae,
country & western, folk, jazz, opera,
hip-hop, rap, show tunes,
religious, spiritual, gospel, new age,
rock, blues

Famous American popular singers (living)

Jennifer Lopez, Mariah Carey,
Miley Cyrus, Lindsay Lohan,
Beyonce, Tina Turner, Janet Jackson,
Justin Timberlake, Christina Aguilera,
Jessica Simpson, Lady Ga Ga,
Barbra Streisand, Mary J Blige,
Steven Tyler, Sheryl Crowe,
Patti la Belle, Annie Lennox, Prince,
Dolly Parton, Willie Nelson

HARD

Musical Instruments

Woodwinds: flute, clarinet, oboe, sax(ophone), bassoon

Strings: violin, cello, viola, banjo, bass, guitar, ukulele, lute, harp

Brass: trombone, trumpet, French horn, tuba

Percussion: piano, drums, tambourine, cymbals

Etc: keyboard, accordion, organ, harmonica

Kinds of TV shows or movies (some may apply to both)

TV programs: talk show, game/quiz show, reality TV, soap (opera), cartoon, children's show, news, sports, cooking, nature, shopping, sitcom, weather

Movies/films: animated, anime, historical, comedy, romantic comedy, drama, western, mystery, musical, thriller, action, adventure, documentary, horror, sci fi (science fiction), fairy tale, foreign (subtitles), short subject

EASY

Animal sounds

pig - snort, grunt, oink; pigeon - coo; mice/rats - squeak; birds - cheep, chirp; seals - bark; sheep/lamb - baa, bleat; snakes - hiss; lion/tiger/bear - growl, roar; frog - ribbit, croak; turkey - gobble; whale - sing; bees - buzz; cat - purr, meow; chicken - cluck; rooster - crow, cock-a-doodle-doo; dog - bark, woof, bowwow; donkey - heehaw, bray; horse - neigh, whinny; duck - quack; elephant - trumpet; monkey - chatter, screech; mosquito - whine

Animals at the zoo

alligator, turtle, crocodile, bear, wolf, elephant, giraffe, zebra, snake, deer, seal, monkey, chimpanzee, baboon, gorilla, hippopotamus, rhinoceros, leopard, tiger, lion, sea lion. panda

HARD

Animals you avoid

poisonous snake, porcupine, rat, alligator, spider, scorpion, skunk, octopus, jellyfish, stingray, anaconda, cockroach, mosquito, shark, bee, wasp, yellow jacket, hornet

Animal parts that people don't have

antennas, paws, claws, hooves, fangs, fur/wool, horns, shells, snouts, spots, stripes, tails, wings, scales, gills

Topic 22 ✸ Did You Ever Have a Pet?
Possible Answers

Pets

dog, cat, bird, parakeet, cockatiel,
parrot, canary, fish, turtle, frog,
hamster, gerbil, guinea pig, rabbit,
chinchilla, ferret, iguana, mouse, snake

What dogs hate and what they love

Hate: cats, bath, the mailman,
strangers, thunder, being tied up,
high-pitched noises

Love: go outside, get walked, chase
squirrels/cats, ride in car,
sleep on your bed, treats, people food,
get their ears scratched, be petted,
be praised, chew on/bury bones,
play fetch

**Reasons to put a dog in obedience
school**

not housebroken, barks, growls,
attacks (the mailman), bites,
jumps up on people, chews furniture,
doesn't behave, ignores commands,
runs away, won't walk on leash
properly, chases cats/squirrels,
needs to socialize

How people treat dogs like humans

dress them, sleep with them, take them
in car, take them on vacation,
hug and kiss them, talk to them,
give them people food, groom them,
play with them

EASY

HARD

Topic 23 ✳ Play Ball
Possible Answers

Sports played with a ball

baseball, softball, basketball, bowling, football, Ping Pong, pool, billiards, racquetball, tennis, volleyball, squash, field hockey, lacrosse, polo, water polo

Sports played without a ball

archery, badminton, biking, boxing, bullfighting, canoeing, kayaking, car racing, gymnastics, horseback riding, ice hockey, karate, mountain climbing, running, skating, skiing, snorkeling, swimming, surfing, waterskiing, weight lifting, wrestling

Olympic sports

Summer: swimming, diving, water polo, canoe, kayak, cycling, gymnastics, fencing, horseback riding, volleyball, wrestling, field hockey, rugby, sailing, table tennis, taekwondo, tennis, triathlon, weight lifting

Winter: bobsleigh, skating, alpine skiing, Nordic skiing, snowboarding, ski jumping, ice hockey, luge

Water and snow sports

Water: sailing, canoeing, rowing, kayaking, rafting, swimming, snorkeling, scuba diving, windsurfing, waterskiing, fishing

Snow: downhill skiing, cross-country skiing, snowboarding, ice skating, sledding, bobsledding, snowmobiling

EASY

HARD

Topic 24 ✹ What Smells Funny?

Possible Answers

EASY

The colors you see

red, pink, orange, yellow, brown, beige, tan, blue, navy blue, baby blue, purple, turquoise, green, black, white, gray, silver, gold

What you smell, nice or not

Nice: buttered popcorn, scented candles, brewed coffee, fruit (pineapple, banana), perfume, lotion, air freshener, talcum powder, herbs and spices (cinnamon, garlic, mint), flowers, oils (eucalyptus, lavender), incense, pine, new car, leather, ocean air

Not nice: ripe garbage, old sponge, wet dog, farts/gas, messy diaper, feet, armpits, gym locker, gasoline, turpentine, pipe/cigar/cigarette smoke, ashtray, sewage, skunk, mothballs, burned food, old fish, bleach, sliced onion, fertilizer, bad breath, some strong smelling cheeses, hairspray, nail polish remover, peroxide (hair dye)

HARD

Things that feel soft

palms of hands, tush/butt, belly, baby's skin, cheek, hair, lips, pillow, stuffed animal, marshmallow, fur, snow, cotton candy, cotton, dough, foam, sand, rose petal, feather, puppies, kittens

Textures

bumpy, smooth, rough, furry, fuzzy, scratchy, silky, soft, slimy, sticky, velvety, spongy, fluffy, rubbery, slippery, greasy, leathery, mushy, prickly (cactus), bristly (beard)

Topic 25 ✳ See No Evil
Possible Answers

Things you see that are red

apple, cherry, strawberry, raspberry, cranberry, red pepper, pimiento, raw meat, tomato, cooked lobster, paprika, radish, watermelon, beets, pomegranate, salsa, red wine, sangria, ketchup, blood, Chinese flag, traffic light (stop), stop sign, Mars, valentines, cardinal (bird), fire engine, fire box, exit sign, ruby, cold cheeks, blushing face

Things that are hot

coffee, tea, hot chocolate, boiling water, steam, soup, potatoes, fire, stove, oven, toaster, iron, tea kettle, the sun, Mercury, Venus, heater, radiator, baseboard, hot sand, desert, light bulb, flat/curling iron, vinyl car seat in summer, coals, barbeque grill, jacuzzi, hot guy/girl

Things that feel sticky

paste, glue, adhesive tape, honey, chewed gum, dried soda on floor, lollipops and candy, maple syrup, leather car seat when it's hot, Post-its, peanut butter, jam, molasses, flypaper, mousetrap, stickers, self-stick stamps, bumper stickers, spider web, tree sap, cotton candy, wet paint, wet cement, frog's tongue

Places and things that are noisy

Places: party, playground, bowling alley, sports arena/stadium, rock concert, daycare center, subway station, bar, casino, amusement park, school cafeteria/ lunchroom, obstetrics ward, hospital nursery, fair

Things: fireworks, gunfire, bomb, volcano, earthquake, snoring, racecar, train, motorcycle, truck, airplane, car horn, chainsaw, jackhammer, highway traffic, siren, cathedral bell, family reunion, alarm clock, smoke detector alarm, battle, boom box, lawn mower, leaf blower, rap music

Possible Answers

EASY

Words associated with a classroom

teacher, aide, desk, chair, computer, movie screen, whiteboard, blackboard, bulletin board, clock, map, globe, PA system, loudspeaker, bookshelves, wastebasket, notebook, binder, pencil, pen, textbook, ruler, calculator

School subjects

Elementary: language arts, social studies, math, science, music, gym

Middle School/ High School: English, math, algebra, geometry, trigonometry, calculus, world/American history, science, biology, chemistry, physics, foreign language, business, typing, bookkeeping, home economics, music, art, computer science, government, economics, driver's education

HARD

Kinds of schools

daycare, preschool, nursery, Head Start, elementary school, middle school, high school, community college, college, university, graduate school, law school, medical school, public school, private school, parochial school, charter school, vocational/technical/trade school, specialized schools - the blind/the deaf

Rooms and places at school

main office, principal's office, nurse's office, guidance office, classroom, art room, music room, hallway, lockers, science lab, gym, locker room, auditorium, cafeteria, library, track, field, bleachers, custodian's closet

Possible Answers

EASY

Words that end in -TION

abbreviation, addition, attention, celebration, circulation, connection, cooperation, education, imagination, invention, motion, multiplication, nation, population, position, production, relation, section, sensation, situation, solution, translation

Words that rhyme with "FIGHT"

bite, bright, delight, excite, flight, fright, height, invite, kite, knight, light, might, mite, night, polite, quite, right, rite, sight, site, slight, spite, tight, tonight, unite

HARD

Other words for "GREAT," as in "That was a great movie."

amazing, awesome, excellent, extraordinary, fabulous, fantastic, impressive, incredible, marvelous, outstanding, remarkable, spectacular, splendid, stupendous, super, terrific, wonderful

Words that rhyme with "YOU"

blue, blew, boo, chew, clue, crew, do, drew, few, flu, glue, grew, knew, new, pew, screw, stew, strew, threw, through, to, too, two, true, view, who, zoo

Possible Answers

EASY

Words that begin with BR-

bracelet, brag, braid, brain, branch, brat, brave, bread, break, breakfast, breathe, brick, bride, bridge, bright, bring, broccoli, broil, broom, brother, brown, brownie, brush

Opposites (big/little)

noisy/quiet, open/closed, right/wrong, rough/smooth, go/stop, day/night, front/back, full/empty, cheap/expensive, clean/dirty, easy/difficult, easy/hard, empty/full, fast/slow, fat/thin, tall/short, up/down, over/under, front/back, before/after, full/empty, hot/cold, happy/sad, dark/light, on/off, near/far, more/less

HARD

Verbs with "UP"

wake up, speak up, shut up, eat up, call up, warm up (leftovers), clean up, lock up, line up, work up (an appetite), think up, dress up, give up, clear up, mess up, wrap up, look up, make up, dry up

Punctuation marks

period .
comma ,
apostrophe '
question mark ?
colon :
exclamation point !
parentheses ( )
hyphen -
semicolon ;
quotation marks " "
dash —

EASY

Abbreviations

a.m.	in. ft. yd. mi.
p.m.	oz. lb.
Ave. Rd.	tsp. tbl.
St. Blvd.	c. pt. qt. gal.
dept.	Nov. Dec. Jan.
ESOL	Mon. Tues. Weds.
etc.	
ex.	
M.D.	
misc.	
Mr. Mrs. Ms.	
Dr. Prof.	
PhD.	

Regular past tense -ed sounds of t/d/id

/t/ asked, brushed, cashed, checked, cooked, coughed, crashed, dressed, fixed, helped, kicked, leaked, looked, marked, mixed, parked, passed, polished, reached, relaxed, rocked, scratched, stretched, talked, walked, waxed, worked

/d/ answered, appeared, boiled, burned, carpooled, cleaned, cleared, combed, covered, delivered, designed, entered, explained, fastened, followed, formed, ironed, learned, listened, lowered, mowed, obeyed, peeled, played, poured, registered, repaired, returned, shortened, signed, spelled, swallowed, turned

/id/ acted, added, assisted, attended, collected, constructed, corrected, deposited, dusted, ended, fainted, folded, guarded, handed, invented, loaded, painted, planted, printed, recorded, repeated, responded, rested, selected, sorted, twisted, vomited

HARD

Irregular past participles with "have/has" such as "have gone" (different from past)

beaten, become, been, begun, broken, chosen, come, done, drawn, driven, drunk, eaten, fallen, flown, given, gone, gotten, grown, known, run, seen, sung, spoken, swum, taken, thrown, woken, written

Adjectives that end with -LESS

ageless, breathless, careless, childless, clueless, effortless, endless, expressionless, harmless, heartless, helpless, humorless, meaningless, odorless, painless, penniless, powerless, restless, senseless, shameless, sleepless, sugarless, tasteless, thankless, thoughtless, tireless, toothless, useless

EASY

Cleaning supplies and equipment

vacuum, broom, mop, feather duster,
dust cloth, rags, sponge, scouring pad,
sponge, paper towels, dustpan,
bucket, pail, window cleaner,
dishwasher liquid, furniture polish,
oven cleaner

Things in the bathroom

vanity, sink, soap dish, faucet,
medicine cabinet, mirror, towel rack,
towels, washcloth, toothbrush holder,
toothbrushes, hamper, hair dryer,
toilet, plunger, toilet brush

HARD

Considerations when buying a house

age of house, size, school district,
interest rate, price, resale value,
condition, location, a basement,
convenient to work and shopping,
peaceful, low-crime neighborhood,
neighbors, be near family, storage,
garage, a yard

Reasons to live in a town (not a city)

tranquil, peaceful, less stressful,
not as noisy, safe, less crime, friendly,
no crowds, fewer lines, less traffic,
easy parking, see nature, night sky,
greenery, trees, less expensive, lower
taxes, less pollution

EASY

What families save money for

emergency, retirement, house,
repairs, vacation, car, college education,
pay bills, security, additions,
new furniture/appliances

Family members

brother, sister, sibling, father, dad,
mother, mom, daughter, son, child,
father/mother/son/daughter-in-law,
in-laws, half brother/sister, aunt, uncle,
cousin, grandmother, grandfather,
grandson, granddaughter, husband,
wife, niece, nephew, step parent,
step child

HARD

**The most important things to look for
in a marriage/relationship**

love, romance, trust, honesty,
communication, respect, equality,
values, wanting children or not,
religious compatibility

What couples argue about

finances, money, in-laws, raising
children, communication, religion,
housework, chores, jealousy, sex,
infidelity, politics, bad habits,
TV remote, TV programs, vacation
destinations

Possible Answers

EASY

Toys

doll, ball, puzzle, stuffed animal, action figures, model cars, trucks, construction toys, blocks, bike, jump rope, roller skates, yo-yo, water pistol, squirt gun, chemistry set, rattle, hula hoop, matchbox cars, video games, model kit, walkie-talkie, bubbles

What you do with a baby

comfort, hold, hug, kiss, cuddle, rock, bounce, carry, sing to (lullaby), give pacifier to, walk in stroller, put in crib to nap/sleep, diaper, bathe, put in a swing, feed, nurse, give bottle, dress, read to, play with

HARD

What a child wants before bed
Why they wake their parents

Wants: water, kiss, hug, go to bathroom, pray, a story, stay up longer, teddy bear

Wake up parents: thirsty, wet bed, scared of thunder, ill, nightmare, go to bathroom, can't sleep

What children don't like
or are scared of

Don't like: homework, the opposite sex, naps, baths, vegetables, kisses, sharing toys, bedtime, naptime, cleaning up

Scared of: shots, thunderstorms, the dark, monsters, the boogey man, seeing the principal, the dentist, the doctor

EASY

Stores

bakery, book, carpet, clothing, computer, department store, drugstore/pharmacy, electronics, fabric, florist, furniture, antiques, grocery/supermarket, hardware, hobby, craft, ice cream, jewelry, music, shoe, thrift, second-hand, toy

Things at a mall that are not stores

food court/restaurant, directory, escalator, elevator, kiosk, info booth, security guard, movie theater, ATM, phone booth, restroom, bench

HARD

Places that offer services

appliance repair, auto repair/garage, bank, barber shop, beauty parlor, car rental, clinic, copy center, DMV (Dept. of Motor Vehicles), dry cleaner, employment agency, eye care center, fire department, funeral parlor, gas station, hospital, IRS (Internal Revenue Service), laundromat, law firm, library, police department, post office, real estate agency, shoe repair shop, tanning salon, tax preparation agency, travel agency, TV/cable

What comes in a box, a jar, and a can

Box: cereal, cookies, spaghetti, chocolates, a cake, pizza, crackers, doughnuts, tea, Jello, aluminum foil wrap, plastic wrap, a gift, tissues

Jar: mayonnaise, jam and jelly, mustard, pickles, tomato sauce, peanut butter, olives

Can: soup, tuna, beans, soda, beer, hair spray, motor oil, tennis balls, shaving cream

EASY

Terms for giving directions

go straight (until), turn left/right, take the first/second street on the left/right, it's opposite the _, it's near/next to/between, at the end of the block, on the corner of/at the intersection of, at the light, around the corner, take the first exit, go north/south, it's about a mile, continue, you'll pass, straight ahead

Types of vehicles with wheels

Cars - sedan, hatchback, convertible, sports car, hybrid, station wagon, minivan, van, SUV, jeep, taxi, truck, pickup truck, dump truck, limo(usine), RV (recreational vehicle/camper), tractor trailer, motorcycle, moped, golf cart, bicycle/bike, train, bus, plane/jet, helicopter

HARD

Kinds of transportation without wheels

boat, ship, canoe, kayak, submarine, raft, sailboat, ferry, cruise ship, ocean liner, rowboat, blimp, hot-air balloon, rocket, sled, toboggan, snowmobile, chairlift, gondola, monorail, parachute, horse, camel

What people don't like about flying

fear of crashing, turbulence, long security line, waiting for flight to take off, uncomfortable seating, crying babies, no food, paying for extras (food, luggage), small bathrooms

EASY

What you wear or take to the beach

bathing suit, shorts, t-shirt, tank top, hat, cap, sunglasses, beach chair, goggles, fins, snorkel, picnic lunch, cooler, suntan lotion, blanket, towels, frisbee, beach ball, float, tube, pail and shovel

Sports wear

gym/basketball/track/running/jogging shoes, shorts, t-shirt, jersey, shin guard, cleats, spikes, shoulder pads, helmet, face mask, sweat band, cup, jockstrap, skates, skis, ski mask, balaclava, ski hat, ski boots, gloves, mittens, earmuffs, windbreaker, jacket, ski jacket

HARD

Kinds of shoes

sneakers, running shoes, tennis shoes, sandals, flip-flops, boots, hiking boots, work boots, cowboy boots, moccasins, slippers, ballet slippers, tap shoes, clogs, loafers, bowling shoes, dress shoes, golf shoes, (football) cleats, flats, high heels, stiletto heels, pumps

Fabrics and materials

leather, suede, denim, silk, satin, velvet, cotton, linen, lace, nylon, cashmere, wool, polyester, corduroy, flannel, rayon, knit, seersucker, spandex, canvas, gauze

EASY

Adjectives that describe people physically

tall/short/average height, heavy/fat/obese/average weight, thin, slender, skinny, long/shoulder length/short/straight/wavy/curly hair, bald, blind, deaf, hearing impaired, handicapped, tattooed, pretty, beautiful, handsome, good looking, blond, brunette, redhead

Adjectives that describe food

delicious, yummy, tasty, yucky, disgusting, inedible, crunchy, greasy, sour, sweet, spicy, hot, cold, salty, bitter, tart, creamy, chewy, juicy, fresh, fishy, messy, gooey, nutritious, raw, ripe, stale, bland, tough

HARD

Positive and negative adjectives that describe people's personalities

Positive: artistic, bashful, shy, quiet, reserved, cheerful, clever, courteous, polite, enthusiastic, friendly, easygoing, funny, humorous, generous, helpful, hard working, honest, kind, lovable, optimistic, pleasant, sensitive, sentimental, sincere, sympathetic

Negative: conceited, mean, cruel, crazy, moody, nervous, impolite, pessimistic, ill-mannered, rude, vain, stuck-up, lazy, sarcastic, judgmental, selfish, negative

Adjectives that describe emotions – How do you feel?

Positive: happy, cheerful, content, delighted, exhilarated, joyful, enthusiastic, excited, relaxed, calm, relieved, hopeful, passionate, confident, brave, courageous

Negative: annoyed, grouchy, irritated, mad, angry, furious, unhappy, sad, moody, depressed, upset, worried, nervous, tense, stressed, ashamed, embarrassed, scared/afraid/frightened, terrified, anxious, apprehensive, tired, exhausted, weary, bored, confused, frustrated, disappointed, lonely, homesick, disgusted, shocked, horrified

EASY

What you can get a traffic ticket for

speeding, expired license/inspection/ registration, DUI (driving under the influence/drunk driving), failure to stop at light/stop sign, not yielding, parking illegally/expired meter, not signaling, not wearing seatbelt, texting while driving

Important documents and cards

birth certificate, adoption certificate, death certificate, passport, visa, green card, will, marriage license, home/ health/car insurance, social security, driver's license, deed/title to house

HARD

Crimes

assault and battery, arson, assassination, murder, homicide, breaking and entering, robbery, theft, burglary, holdup, embezzlement, mugging, car jacking, forgery, fraud, kidnapping, drug dealing, prostitution, rape, smuggling, vandalism, shoplifting

Phrases and words associated with a courtroom

stand trial, read verdict, be pronounced innocent/guilty, be acquitted, let out on bail, be sentenced/convicted, be released (to custody of parents), judge, jury, witness, defendant, prosecuting/defense lawyer/attorney, evidence, DNA testing, guard, court reporter, handcuffs

Possible Answers

EASY

What you see when you look up

sky, sun, moon, stars, rainbow, clouds, comet, meteor, falling star, constellation, Milky Way, skywriting, birds, planes, trees

What people do in their backyards

garden, barbecue, grill, mow lawn, (children) play, play lawn games (badminton, croquet, bocce), play catch, swim, swing, dry clothes, chat with next-door neighbor, rake, sunbathe, entertain, relax

HARD

Flowers and trees

Flowers: mum, crocus, daffodil, geranium, iris, lily, marigold, rose, snapdragon, sunflower, tulip, zinnia, daisy, pansy, petunia, orchid, rose, tulip, violet, hibiscus

Trees: beech, birch, dogwood, maple, oak, palm, spruce, poplar, pine, (weeping) willow, magnolia, fruit, apple, lemon, orange, peach, plum, pear, cherry

Things outside a house and in the yard

mailbox, driveway, sidewalk, porch, front steps, storm/screen door, doorbell, front door, door knocker, window, shutter, roof, garage, patio, garage door, lawn furniture, shed, lawnmower, gardening tools, deck, compost heap, barbecue grill, gutter, drainpipe, TV antenna, satellite dish, doghouse, bird feeder, bird bath, chimney, fence/gate, shovel, spade, hoe, rake, hose, pump, sprinkler

EASY

Languages

English, French, Chinese, Arabic, Farsi, German, Greek, Haitian Creole, Hindi, Hebrew, Italian, Japanese, Korean, Polish, Portuguese, Russian, Spanish, Swahili, Swedish, Tagalog, Thai, Turkish, Urdu, Vietnamese

European countries

Austria, Belgium, Czech Republic, Denmark, England/Great Britain, Finland, France, Germany, Greece, Ireland, Italy, Luxembourg, Netherlands, Norway, Poland, Russia, Spain, Sweden, Switzerland, Turkey

HARD

International capital cities

Canada - Ottawa; Czech Republic - Prague; Ecuador - Quito; Egypt - Cairo; France - Paris; Germany - Berlin; Greece - Athens; Haiti - Port au Prince; Hungary - Budapest; India - New Delhi; Iran - Tehran; Ireland - Dublin; Peru - Lima; Japan - Tokyo; South Korea - Seoul; Mexico - Mexico City; Poland - Warsaw; Portugal - Lisbon; Spain - Madrid; Thailand - Bangkok; Turkey - Ankara; USA - Washington, DC; Vietnam - Hanoi; Venezuela - Caracas

Countries ending with -LAND

England, Finland, Greenland, Holland, Iceland, Ireland, New Zealand, Poland, Scotland, Swaziland, Switzerland, Thailand

EASY

What parents remind or encourage do children to do

their homework, study, be honest/ truthful, be kind/nice/polite, sit up straight, be neat, clean room, read, wash hands, brush teeth, use the bathroom, tie shoes, eat vegetables, go to bed, turn off the lights, call them on phone, practice musical instrument, do chores

Things made of plastic

bags, food containers, shower curtains, silverware/plates/cups, CD cases, milk containers, soda bottles, baby bottles, pens, remote controls, light switches, credit cards, toys, helmets, medicine bottles, keyboards, straws, toothbrush

HARD

Things that have changed since Grandma's time

technological advances - computers, email, skype, internet, GPS, DVD's, cell phones, global warming, cable TV, reality TV, 3D movies, the price of gas, women in the workplace, credit cards, hairstyles and fashion, attitude toward smoking, hybrid/electric cars, disposable diapers, online classes, appliances

Objects and Events that Bring Good and Bad Luck

Good luck: four-leaf clover, horseshoe, lucky rabbit's foot, throw salt over shoulder, finding a penny, knock on wood, wish on a wishbone, blow out birthday candles, cross your fingers, wear garlic, the color red, bride wears something old/new/borrowed/blue

Bad luck: black cat crosses your path, groom sees bride before wedding, cattle lying down means rain, going under ladder, breaking a mirror, number 13, Friday the 13th, opening an umbrella in the house

EASY

HARD

Expansion Activities

Alternate Individual Play

Individually (not as a group) students are given time to generate words. When they are done, write a composite of their answers on the board. To limit the amount of board work, you may have to keep the time limit short.

The students get a point for every answer they have which is on the board. (In this game, students get a point for having the same answer, as well as TWO points for their own unique answers.)

Then you can go into groups. Have them try to generate additional words. For each unique answer a group has, each student in that group adds a point to their individual score. Candy for the winning person.

A Cooperative Game (everybody wins)

Groups of students are given the same card and a time limit. They write their answers on the card and then copy their list on a piece of paper. When done, the groups exchange cards. They add new words they hadn't thought of to their list, get a new card, and add more words to their list, until all the lists are complete and the same. A student reads the composite list, and it is posted for further reference. You can use the Answer Key to supplement the list.

Expanding into a Lesson

A picture dictionary is a wonderful resource for all levels, including Advanced, who are often deemed 'past that.' It can be the basis for this expansion activity. Many of the topics in *Got It!* can be found in a picture dictionary (Kitchen, Weather, Fruit, Body), though the subtopic prompts on the cards may reflect a twist.

After playing **Got It!** using a topic found in a dictionary and after compiling a common list on the board, hand out one dictionary per group, marking the relevant page for that topic (or a copy of the page). The students find the words they 'got.' Then they find the ones they missed. You can leave the list up for beginners, adding the new words, or erase the board so the students need to recall their lists. Discuss new vocabulary, using the visuals as a cue. Topics can lead to discussion. ("What's your favorite appliance? Why? How much time do you spend in the kitchen?")

Students' answers can be checked for spelling and used for pronunciation practice. Any topic can lend itself to grammar. Nouns can be pluralized (with the sounds of /s/ /z/ or /iz/. Verbs can be put into the past tense, and divided into regular and irregular verbs. Regular verbs can be charted as to the pronunciation of the -ed suffix (/d/ /t/ /id/).

Chitchat

No matter how advanced, ESOL students always seem to want practice talking. Many of the topics lend themselves to further **chitchat**. After playing the game, students are in oral mode, warmed up, and have generated relevant vocabulary. The following are examples of how to expand a topic; other ideas may come to you as you play the game.

Topic 1 *Easy* 1   Have you always worn your hair this way? (when you were younger?)

Topic 1 *Hard* 2   What is a bad habit that bothers you?

Topic 2 *Hard* 2   What kind of wedding did you have/do you want?

Topic 3 *Hard* 1   Did you ever quit a job? Why?

Topic 5, 6   Do you eat differently since coming to the U.S.?

Topic 10 *Hard* 2   Have you ever experienced a natural disaster, or known someone who has?

Topic 12 *Hard* 2   Do you or someone you know have any fears?

Topic 16 *Easy* 2   What's your weekend typically like?

Topic 16 *Hard* 1   What do you do for entertainment?

Topic 17 *Hard* 1   Have you been to D.C.? What is your impression of it?

Topic 26   Did/do you like school? Did/do you have a favorite subject?

Topic 30 *Hard* 1   What was the most important thing for you when looking for a place to live?

Topic 31 *Hard* 2   Do you want to tell us what you and your spouse/mother/sibling argue about?

Topic 34 *Easy* 1   Give oral directions from here to your house. Use the terms in the Answer Key.

Topic 34 *Hard* 2   Who flew for the first time coming to the U.S.? What was it like for you?

Topic 37 *Easy* 1   Have you ever gotten a traffic ticket? What was that experience like?

Students can chat among themselves in their group and all will get a chance to speak. Or you can lead this as a whole-group activity, the advantage being that you can monitor and model correctly what they say. You don't want to over-correct them when they're expressing themselves; it can inhibit them. However, they seem to appreciate some correction. Try not to let the more assertive students dominate; the quiet ones often run deep and deserve a chance to speak.

Debate

The topics on some cards can be adapted for oral **debate**, such as the ones below.

Topic 3 *Easy* 1   Should students wear uniforms?

Topic 4 *Hard* 2   Do you believe teenagers should work?

Topic 4   Do you think women should work after they have children?

Topic 7 *Hard* 2   Many people start to eat fast food when they come to the U.S. Do you think it's a good thing?

Topic 11 *Easy* 2   Is it better do take medicine or to do natural cures for things like headaches, stomach aches, colds, etc.?

Topic 16 *Easy* 1   Should men and women equally share household chores?

Topic 22 *Hard* 2   Would you have a dog live indoors and treat it "like a human"?

Topic 30 *Hard* 2   Would you prefer to live in a city rather than a small town?

Topic 34   Would you or your spouse commute an hour or more each way to work?

After playing **Got It!** have students divide into groups according to how they answer these questions. In their new groups, assign a more advanced student to take notes on their reasons – the pros or cons, advantages or disadvantages.

Note: Note taking is a skill, and students should know that notes needn't be "perfect" (spelling or neatness, and no white out!) and they should shorten sentences to phrases.
Ex: "Fast food is not healthy because you can gain a lot of weight."
  not healthy – gain weight

See if students can group related ideas and eliminate the unnecessary.

After generating a list of ideas, it is time for the debate. Simply have individuals in opposing groups take turns going back and forth in counter-argument. Arguments can sometimes get heated or perhaps go off on a tangent, and you will need to act as moderator. But they are often lively and will engage your language learners in relevant communication.

Writing

Segueing from **debate to writing** will help to eliminate the dread some students feel toward this skill. Writing will not loom as such a challenge as they have already generated ideas in discussion and have notes on it. So, for example, some students will write about "Why it's Better to Live in a City."

If your students aspire to GED or college, a standard five-paragraph essay with an introduction, a three-paragraph body, and a conclusion is appropriate. Otherwise, you can just let them write about what they have already discussed without dictating a format. You will want to teach them paragraph form if they are not familiar with it (and many students are not).

It's a good idea to start them off writing in class where you're available to help (and check that they have actually begun the process), and let them complete it at home at their own pace. Have them read it over before submitting; does it sound right? They will find mistakes. Correct their papers judiciously, i.e. pick and choose errors. You will note they will tend to make the same errors in writing that they make orally. Perhaps you can get them to rewrite the paper reflecting corrections, and read some aloud.

Below are some **prompts that can be adapted to writing that would not require debate.** Instead, they might use the words that were generated in the game, or that are found in the Answer Key, as a foundation for writing.

Topic 2 *Hard* 2   Write about a memorable wedding – yours or someone else's. Use the vocabulary you have brainstormed or the vocabulary in the Answer Key.

Topic 3 *Hard* 2   Which of these jobs would you most like for yourself/spouse/child? Why?

Topic 10 *Hard* 1   Use some of the weather terms you listed to write about your favorite kind of weather and how it makes you feel. You can use the adjectives from Topic 36 H2.

Topic 16 *Hard* 2   Write about a hobby or craft you do or did.

Topic 17 *Easy* 1   Write about your favorite American holiday, or one in your country.

Topic 36 *Easy* 1 *Hard* 1   Describe someone you know. Use the adjectives to describe them physically and their personality.

Topic 36 *Hard* 2   How did you feel about coming to the U.S. before you came? And now? Use the adjectives that describe emotions.

Topic 40 *Easy* 1   What were you taught to do when you were a child? What do you encourage your children to do? Use the vocabulary you brainstormed or the Answer Key.

Writing for Lower-Level Students

Lower-level students can practice writing sentences on any topic. After having generated lists, or using the words in the Answer Key, have them simply choose ten words to write about.

So **Topic 3 *Hard* 2** (Occupations) might produce:

1. My favorite actor is Leonardo DiCaprio.
2. An appliance repair person came to my house and fixed the refrigerator.
3. Sometimes I get a babysitter for my kids when my husband and I go out.

Or **Topic 6 *Easy* 2** :

1. My coffee maker is my favorite appliance.
2. I never had a trash compactor before.
3. I do not use a microwave.

Try **Topic 9 *Easy* 1** and ***Easy* 2**, **Topic 10 *Easy* 1**, **Topic 13 *Hard* 2**, **Topic 16 *Easy* 1**, ***Easy* 2**, and ***Hard* 1** (etc.) for words that lend themselves to sentence writing.

Other Books from Pro Lingua on Games and Vocabulary

Match It! A photocopyable teacher resource. 83 sets of games based on the popular game "Concentration." Approximately half of the games can be done by beginners.

Index Card Games for ESL. A photocopyable teacher resource with dozens of games, from easy to difficult. Copy, cut, and paste on index cards.

Superphonic Bingo. 15 photocopyable games following the presentation of sound-letter combinations in *From Sound to Sentence*. Each game has 8 different cards and two incomplete cards.

Lexicarry. All Levels. A vocabulary builder that features over 2500 captionless pictures. An English word list is in the back of the book, and word lists in ten other languages are available as booklets or free on the web. The illustrations are grouped into Communicative Functions, Sequences, Related Actions, Operations, Topics, Places, and Proverbs and Sayings.

Getting a Fix on Vocabulary. A student text and CD that focuses on word building through affixation – prefixes and suffixes – and learning common Latin and Greek roots. The vocabulary is presented in the context of newspaper articles and radio news broadcasts, and practiced in a variety of exercises. Intermediate and Advanced.

A to Z Picture Activities: Phonics and Vocabulary for Emerging Readers. In each unit, one letter of the alphabet is examined for the sounds it can make and illustrations of words that make those sounds. Additionally, each unit contains illustrated vocabulary of specific topic areas, such as animals, body, colors, days, eating, etc.

Go Fish. A collection of 86 pairs of brightly colored vocabulary cards showing pictures of things you would find in a home. In addition to the Go Fish game, six other games are explained. Suitable for beginners.

Shenanigames: Grammar-Focused Activities and Games. 49 games with 96 pages of photocopyable masters. Each game focuses on a grammar point, such as adjective (relative) clauses, comparatives, noun clauses, tag questions, etc.

The Learner's Lexicon. A list of 2400 words arranged in four levels; 300 (limited survival), 600 (surviving), 1200 (adjusting), and 2400 (participating). A reference for those developing their own lessons and curricula.

For more information or to order, go to www.ProLinguaAssociates.com
or call 800-366-4775